M000317991

READY,
SET,
BRAND!

THE CANVA FOR WORK
QUICKSTART GUIDE

LISA LARSON-KELLEY

Beginners Brain Publishing
Ready, Set, Brand! The Canva for Work Quickstart Guide
Lisa Larson-Kelley

Copy Editors: Martina Kunar, Hannah Field
Cover Design: Lisa Larson-Kelley
Interior Design: Amber Medel
Production Assistance: Michelle Racca
Design and Content Contributions: Canva Design School (https://designschool.canva.com)

Published in the United States by Beginners Brain Publishing
ISBN 978-0-9968054-0-7

Version 1.0
http://learnfromlisa.com/ready-set-brand

Contents

Foreword

Welcome to the Visual Content Revolution!

Today there are over 2 billion active social media accounts globally.* That's a lot of people to reach – a lot of potential customers. It's an amazing time to be a marketer, isn't it?!

Wait, you're not a marketer, you say? Well, you may not think of yourself as one, but in our fast-paced always-connected world we ALL need to be marketers.

Unfortunately, not all of us have the time, skills, and know-how to put together visual materials that are both beautiful and effective. People with brilliant minds for copy are expected to pick an appropriate typeface and put that copy into an Instagram image. Someone with a deep understanding of statistics needs to create an infographic. It's crazy, really...

This is why I've fallen in love with Canva.

Canva removes the barriers of learning complicated software and making sophisticated design decisions -- letting you create visuals using pre-built and customizable templates with a drag-and-drop interface. It's nothing short of revolutionary. It's such a game-changer that I just had to write a book to help spread the word!

SOURCE: We Are Social, Jan. 2015, http://www.lisa.fyi/wearesocial

Changing the rules

One of the earliest lessons I learned in my career as a graphic designer was the old adage: "Fast, good and cheap. Pick two." This concept will be

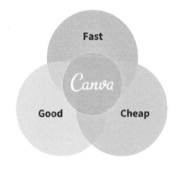

familiar to anyone who has ever felt the pressure of delivering visual marketing with limited resources.

This is why I love Canva for Work so much. It defies this principle -- making it possible to have all three! With a little upfront work to configure your brand kit, your team will have the freedom to start creating, knowing that their visual marketing is supporting your brand. They don't need to worry if they're making the right design choices -- and neither do you!

Why you need this book

I wrote this book to be an essential companion and reference for Canva for Work -- helping you get up and running fast, and work efficiently.

I've always loved breaking down technology into digestible, understandable bits, and helping people see every problem as solvable and not intimidating. In fact, back when I was working in the print shop as a designer, my coworkers always came to me when they needed to know the size of an A3 envelope, or how many 3"x5" postcards could be printed from a 12x18 sheet of paper, or the best place to find embossed card stock... I had the answers because I kept a notebook full of notes from past projects. They called it "Lisa's brain" and I was diligent in keeping it up to date and expanded it with what I had learned from every new project. And I loved to share that knowledge.

This is what I offer in this book -- an organized reference and instruction manual for Canva for Work -- for designers and non-designers alike. It will give you everything you need to make the most of your investment.

Hit the ground running

As early adopters such as Upworthy, Techcrunch, and Yelp have discovered, Canva for Work is powerful yet so easy to set up and learn that you can start creating beautiful branded designs literally in minutes. Now, it's your turn. I can't wait to see what you create!

Lisa Larson-Kelley

Chapter 1:
How Canva is Changing Design in the Workplace

Back in 2007, Melanie Perkins, CEO and Co-Founder of Canva, had a dream. She dreamt of empowering everyone to create beautiful designs without friction – and without the need to learn complicated software. She envisioned a tool that would guide people to create more beautiful designs in the right dimensions, with gorgeous typography and images.

Today, that dream is a reality. As of this writing, more than 4 million people are using Canva to make beautiful graphics for the web and for print. Canva has rapidly grown to become the go-to platform for non-designers and designers alike to create visual content.

With this cloud-based web and iPad app, you can pick a template, choose a style, drag and drop type and images then quickly save and download the file. You can create a wide variety of visual content such as presentations, social media graphics, posters and more.

Canva is remarkably simple to use. But as more and more companies and power users have started using Canva, there has been demand for enhanced productivity and team collaboration features. The Canva team listened – and Canva for Work was born.

How Canva for Work Makes Canva More Awesome

In the recent past, graphic designers needed to touch everything and anything visual if you wanted it to look professional. People who were not professional designers were forced to use hacked-together online tools or throw something together in Powerpoint to get something out the door, searching online or guessing at accurate sizes for social media graphics or printing specs.

> *In a recent survey of 500 SME business owners in the U.S., 78% of companies said that people who are not professional designers create social media graphics, customer facing presentations, and other marketing materials.*

Canva for Work is changing all of that. With this revolutionary tool, your whole team can work together, with access to the same branding design elements, templates, colors, and fonts – allowing you to collaborate to create consistent visual content.

This approach has the potential to completely transform the way your company works internally. Rather than having a designer create a one-off design, they can create a template that everyone in the company can easily edit, add their own text, swap out images, and share with the world. You're free from having to learn and license complicated design software, and you can be confident your visual content is the right size and is always consistent with your brand.

Time to Get to Work!

This book was written to give you everything you need to become a Canva for Work power user. I'll walk you through initial account setup, populating your Brand Kit, creating templates, and sharing your visuals with your team and with the world. Along the way you'll learn best practices and productivity tricks that will help you maximize your investment in Canva for Work. The platform allows you to complete tasks such as resize multiple designs, save a brand kit, invite your team to collaborate and much more. You'll become familiar with common graphics terms and standards – and have everything at your fingertips, all in one place. I've even included a reference card in the back of the book that you can either tear out (if you have the printed book) or print out (if you have the ebook) and keep next to your desk for quick access to keyboard shortcuts in Canva.

Whether you're a seasoned professional designer or a marketer who's been thrust into the designer role -- you're about to experience a revolution in the way you work.

Let's get started!

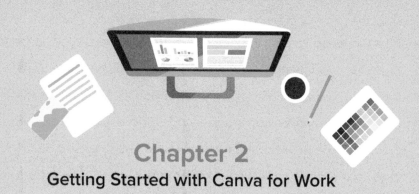

Chapter 2
Getting Started with Canva for Work

Canva is an amazing free tool. Its features are optimized to meet a specific need — to quickly and easily create attractive graphics at the right sizes for social media and print, without requiring sophisticated design skills or high-end software. If you've been using it for awhile, you've probably been able to bend it to your will. But I'll bet you have a secret wish list of features that would make your life SO. MUCH. EASIER. Features like:

- ✪ Magically resizing designs, allowing you to create consistent graphics across all of your social media platforms automatically

- ✪ Consistent default fonts for headlines, subheads, and body copy

- ✪ Default brand colors so you don't need to keep looking them up (or saving that sticky note on your monitor!)

- ✪ Sharable folders for photos and brand graphics

- ✪ Ability to create and save easy-to-customize brand templates that you and your team can use to create new projects.

If you've been waiting and hoping for these productivity boosting features — your wait is over. You are simply going to love Canva for Work. Not only does it give you a Brand Kit for consistent fonts, colors and graphics, but you can work more easily as a team to build creative visual content for your brand. And getting started is easy. In this chapter, I'll walk you through upgrading your Canva account to Canva for Work, give you a tour of the features, and introduce you to the team stream so you've got the lay of the land and you're ready to get working.

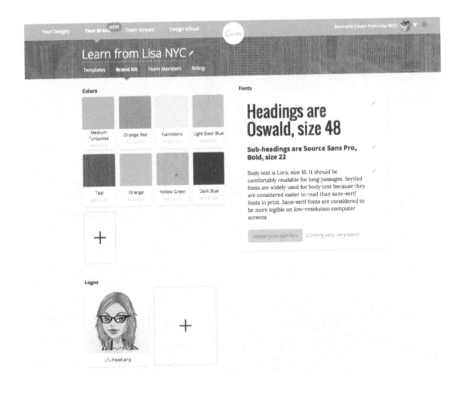

Creating a Canva for Work Account

If you've already started using Canva for free, you can upgrade your account to gain access to Canva for Work. At a price point of US$9.95 per user per month (annual subscription) or US$12.95 per user per month paying monthly, Canva for Work is affordable for small startups or freelancers as well as larger companies. Signing up is easy.

Features & Capabilities	Canva	Canva for Work
Photo straightening & cropping tools	X	X
Text, text holders & speech bubbles	X	X
Stock photos	X	X
Shapes and icons	X	X
Photo frames and grids	X	X
Transparent backgrounds	X	X
Photo filters	X	X
Customizable templates	X	X
Stickers & badges	X	X
Save brand colors, logos & fonts		X
Resize designs		X
Save brand templates		X
Organize images into folders		X
Share photo folders with your team		X
Create brand templates		X
Share designs with Team Stream		X
Access controls for teams		X

Coming soon on Canva for Work

⭐ Upload your own fonts
⭐ Commenting
⭐ Full iPad support

STEPS TO SIGN UP

1 Go to **Canva.com/work** and look for the button to sign up

or "upgrade now." You'll be prompted to either create a new account or to sign in to an existing Canva account. If you choose to login to an existing account here, you'll be able to use that login  to access both your free personal account and your Canva for Work account and toggling between them is easy.

2 After you log in or create a new account, you'll be prompted to enter your payment information. As part of the registration, you'll receive a free trial though you'll still need to enter your credit card information. You won't be charged until after the trial period ends.

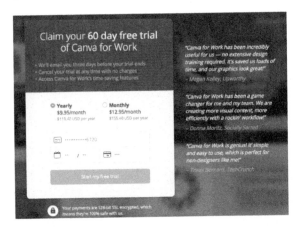

Once you enter your payment info and click Start my free
trial, you can login to Canva for Work immediately and start
creating.

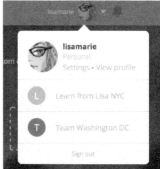

3 From your account dashboard, go
to the upper right corner of your
account dropdown menu. Click
on it, and you can access your
various accounts. I have three –
my personal (free) account, my
consultancy (Learn from Lisa) team, and Team Washington DC (a
test team I set up for a workshop). You can be a part of multiple
teams with different brand kits and templates and keep the
assets for each team separate.

That's it! You now have a Canva for Work account and you're ready to
have a look around at the awesome new features you've just unlocked.

Same Interface, Different World

Canva for Work takes the same Canva elements, easy-to-use tools
and interface and opens it up to a different world of collaboration
and teamwork.

The first thing you may notice about the interface is that it feels familiar. In
fact, it's very similar to the free Canva interface, but with some powerful
new options. Let's take a look at what you now have at your fingertips.

New tabs, richer features

Next to the Your Designs tab in the top navigation bar, you now have Your Brand and Team Stream.

YOUR BRAND TAB

Under this tab you'll find the core features of Canva for Work: Templates, Brand Kit, and Team Members, as well as Billing settings.

- ⊛ **Templates.** Empower your team to create professional materials that consistently represent your company's brand. When you create templates for your team they will appear under the Templates tab.

- ⊛ **Brand Kit.** Set colors, fonts, and logos that will be the default for all designs created by your team. This tab is where you'll set up this kit for everyone to use.

- ⊛ **Team Members.** Collaborate with multiple people to create consistent designs for your brand. Under this tab,

you can invite new team members and set their level of access - Administrator, Template Designer, or Member.

✪ **Billing.** Make changes to your plan, cancel your account, view purchase history, or update your payment method for your monthly membership and premium image purchases.

TEAM STREAM

With Canva for Work, you can let others join in on the design process, letting you work together as a team to build creative visual content for your brand. Through the Team Stream, you can see what each of your team members are creating and working on. From here you can choose to edit one of the designs

directly or remix it into a new design of your own.

I'll go into more detail about working with teams in Canva for Work in an upcoming chapter, giving you best practices for managing your team's workflow, using the Team Stream, and more.

Next, let's get your Brand Kit configured!

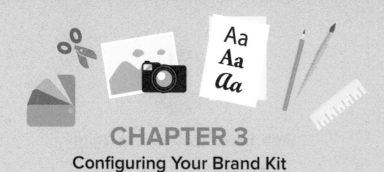

CHAPTER 3
Configuring Your Brand Kit

The Brand Kit is the foundation of Canva for Work. This is where you set up all of the design elements your team will use when creating visuals -- colors, templates, logos and other artwork that they'll use to knock out beautiful designs.

You'll call upon your inner designer (yes, everyone has one), supported by the wealth of resources in Canva's Design School, to set up your Brand Kit. Don't fret -- in this chapter, I'll walk you through each step involved in building this solid foundation for your brand. Once your Brand Kit is configured, your team of designers and non-designers alike will have everything they need to quickly create on-brand visual marketing materials in Canva for Work.

Let's dive in!

Step 1: Set Your Brand Colors

"Color sets a mood, conveys emotions, and defines your style. Brands have long relied on color to say something about them. When selecting a palette, you should think about what emotions or mood you want to communicate."
— *Juily Gite, Staples Design Services*

Colors set the tone and feeling of your brand.

If you're working with an established brand, you likely have specific colors that you need to use across all of your visuals. Even with this list in hand, it can be hard to be sure everyone uses the right colors consistently. Canva realized this, and made it super easy for

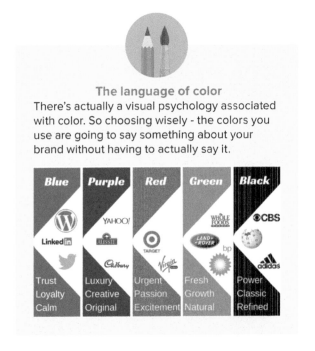

The language of color
There's actually a visual psychology associated with color. So choosing wisely - the colors you use are going to say something about your brand without having to actually say it.

Blue	Purple	Red	Green	Black
Trust	Luxury	Urgent	Fresh	Power
Loyalty	Creative	Passion	Growth	Classic
Calm	Original	Excitement	Natural	Refined

your team to access your brand's official colors for their designs. Everything you need is under the Brand Kit tab in your Canva for Work admin page.

For help choosing colors for your brand, see the Color Theory section of the Canva Design School for a complete guide.

What do you need?

Hex codes for your brand colors

What do you need to do?

1 Open up the Brand Kit tab under the Your Brand tab in your Canva for Work account

2 Assign colors in your Brand Kit

3 Done!

Let's do it.

Adding your brand colors here is as easy as clicking the + icon.

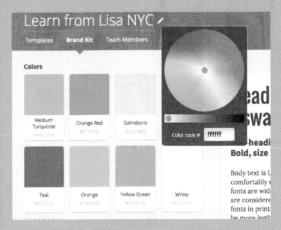

This brings up a color wheel. You can click on the picker and use the tint slider to select the color's hue, or enter a specific HEX value of your desired color in the color code field.

What the heck is a HEX code?

HEX code is a 6-digit code that represents a specific color. It is made up of 2 digits each for the three primary colors that computers recognize – red, green, and blue.

00	00	00
Red	Green	Blue

Hex numbers use 16 digits:
0 1 2 3 4 5 6 7 8 9 A B C D E F

The smallest representation of a color	The greatest intensity of a color

Combinations of these digits create different shades of a particular color. Double zero "00" indicates an absence of that color. FF is equal to a pure color.

So let's take what we now know and figure out how to make the common colors black and white. Consider that computers create colors with light, an additive process. So black would be the total absence of color -- or 000000. And to create the lightest color, white, pure red, green, and blue are added together -- or FFFFFF. Can you guess what color code FF0000 would produce? (answer below)

Pure red.

If you don't know the HEX values of your brand colors, you can use the **Color Picker extension** in Google Chrome to find out the HEX code for any color used on a webpage. Another handy tool is **imagecolorpicker.com**. Here you can upload your company logo or a screenshot of your home page and click on parts of the image to grab the HEX color codes. Simple and easy!

If you already know the RGB value of your color, **hex.colorrrs.com** will tell you the HEX values.

If you're just experimenting with different colors at this point, you can click anywhere on the color wheel and drag the grayscale slider to get just the right color.

Once you've entered all of your brand colors into your Brand Kit, everyone on your Canva for Work team will have them set as their default colors for new designs. Never again will you have visual materials with the wrong shade of green -- everything will be on-color and on-brand!

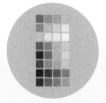

How many colors do you really need?
https://designschool.canva.com/blog/color-tips/

Graphic designers recommend that you avoid using an excessive amount of colors. After all, less is more!

Unless purposely going for a rainbow look, designers say to stick with 3 or 4 colors. This will keep your graphics clean and give your some guidelines while you design, helping you to stay consistent and on-brand.

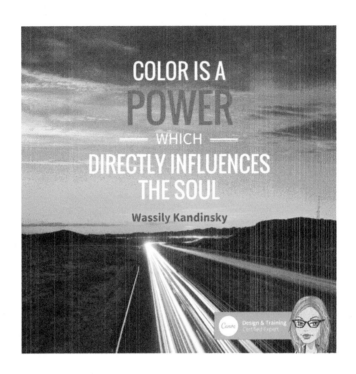

Step 2: Choose your fonts

Next, you'll set the default fonts for headings, sub-headings, and body copy in your designs. Your company likely has a font or group of fonts that you use for all of your marketing materials. Canva gives you a great selection of fonts, but not every font under the sun -- so it's possible you will need to choose one that is closest to your font. At the time of this writing, you cannot upload your own fonts to Canva for Work. (This is a top feature request, however, so I've been assured that feature is coming soon!)

What the font?!

Don't know what font your brand has used in the past, and don't have anyone to ask? Try the useful (and kind of magical) service, What the Font (http://www.myfonts.com/WhatTheFont/). Submit an image to WhatTheFont to find the closest matches in their database, then see if that font exists in Canva. There are also helpful font enthusiasts standing by to lend a hand in the WhatTheFont Forum.

What do you need?

Font names or examples for reference

What do you need to do?

1. Open up the **Brand Kit tab** under the **Your Brand tab** in your Canva for Work account

2. Assign fonts to headings, sub-headings, and body copy

3. Done!

Let's do it.

In your Brand Kit, click on the pencil next to the heading text. A menu will pop up allowing you to choose from the Canva font list, set type size, and choose bold or italic type. Choose your brand's font, or one that is the closest match. These three font selections will appear at the top of the font list for all of your team members, and will be the default fonts for any new text boxes they create in their designs.

10 Golden Rules for choosing fonts:
tips from designer Janie Kliever

01. CHOOSE COMPLEMENTARY FONTS

As is often the case with people, opposites tend to attract: "introverted" and "extroverted" fonts balance each other nicely when combined. So if you have a distinctive font with a "strong personality" (often referred to as a display font), pair it with something more neutral and conservative for a balanced design.

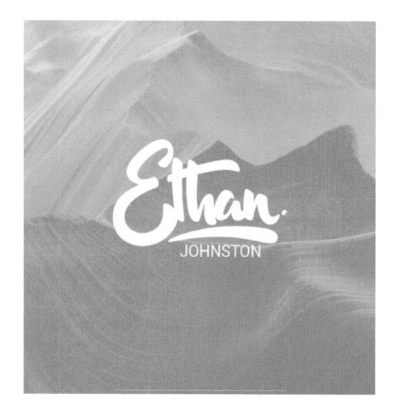

Make a point of noticing how fonts combine well (or not) out "in the wild" — on websites, in magazines, on store signs and product packaging — and you'll start to develop an eye for what works and what doesn't.

02. ESTABLISH A VISUAL HIERARCHY

Combine fonts in way that visually separates different textual elements like headlines, sub-headlines, body copy, and captions. Qualities such as size, boldness (also known as "weight"), and spacing (including leading, the space between lines, and kerning, the space between letters) all contribute to how the eye should navigate the page and what text should attract attention first. Decide what information is essential — what must stand out at first glance (a company name, a headline, a special offer?)—and what is less important.

Then, make your font style, size, and arrangement choices accordingly. The most important textual element is generally (though not always) the largest and the weightiest.

03. CONSIDER CONTEXT

Where your design will appear should help you determine what fonts will work for your project. The text should be easily readable at the size it is going to be displayed. Notice how in the example below, the smallest text is in all caps, and the letters are spaced generously — both choices enhance legibility.

Context can also be approached in terms of genres and historical periods. Do a little research into the backgrounds of the fonts you're considering – when they were used, for what purpose, or even how they've been used in a cultural context. This can help guide you to choose a font with the right aesthetic for your brand.

04. MIX SERIFS AND SANS SERIFS

Running short on time and need to pick two fonts, quick? Try one serif and one sans serif. The two tend to work together well, particularly at contrasting sizes.

05. CREATE CONTRAST

One of the main reasons that pairing serif and sans-serif fonts works so well is that it creates contrast. Contrast can be achieved in a number of ways, including through style, size, weight, spacing, and color, among others. In the example below, a bold, chunky font is paired with a tall, thin one — and although they're almost complete opposites, they work nicely together in large part because they are so different. The differences help create distinct roles for each font, allowing them to stand out as individual pieces of information.

06. STEER CLEAR OF CONFLICT

When combining fonts, you do want contrast, but you don't want conflict. Generally speaking, typefaces that share a couple qualities — maybe they have similar proportions, or the lowercase letters have the same height (known as "x-height") — are more likely to look harmonious together, even if the overall appearance differs.

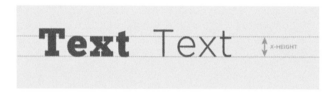

07. AVOID PAIRING FONTS THAT ARE TOO SIMILAR

On the flip side of Rule #5, choosing fonts that are too similar (i.e., don't have enough contrast) becomes problematic. Any differences that are discernible may look more like a mistake than a purposeful choice. Here's an easy way to test whether two or more fonts might be too similar: Place them side by side on your screen, then sit back a little and squint. If the fonts look basically the same, then that's a good indication that your design could benefit from turning up the contrast between your type choices.

08. USE FONTS FROM THE SAME FAMILY

Using typefaces from the same family is always a safe bet; after all, they were created to work together. Look for families that come with a range of options (different weights, styles, cases) to ensure that you have enough variation for your purposes. Limiting your typefaces to one font family streamlines the design process, eliminating the need to decide on the perfect fonts to combine and automatically helps you create a more cohesive look.

09. LIMIT YOUR NUMBER OF FONTS

You may have heard it said that you should keep fonts for one project to only two or three. In fact, in your Canva for Work Brand Kit, you are limited to 3 font choices, Headline, Subhead, and Body copy. That's an appropriate rule of thumb in certain applications (and is common in editorial designs like magazine spreads), but it is by no means a hard-and-fast rule. You may have a need for more elaborate font combinations, such as illustrations or infographics. These you can set up as templates, overriding the Brand Kit defaults. If you do choose to use a variety of fonts, the overall effect should be harmonious, not conflicting or cluttered.

SOM
MAIRE

L'AVENTURE DU MUSCAT 04 - 10
TÉMOIGNAGE
Mme RENÉE CASTALID ET ROMAIN HALL   p 04 - 07

BALMA VENITIA,
UNE CAVE EN AVANCE SUR SON TEMPS   p 08 - 10

**VIGNOBLE
& DÉCOUVERTE** 14 - 17
AUTOUR DES DENTELLES DE MONTMIRAIL   p 14 - 15

LA ROQUE ALRIC,
UNE SENTINELLE AU COEUR DES DENTELLES   p 16 - 17

PAROLES

10. PRACTICE!

Last but not least, a friendly suggestion rather than a rule: Practice combining fonts on your own, when there's not money or your boss' good opinion riding on the project. As with any skill, becoming competent involves a lot of trial-and-error. So take risks. Experiment. Use your intuition. Sometimes you'll just have a feeling that something works, even if it technically shouldn't, according to the "rules." Other times, you'll just know that a font pairing isn't working; try to figure out why and learn from it. Take these typography basics as a starting point, and if they serve you well, use them — if not, don't let them stifle your creativity.

Excerpted from Canva Design School, "10 Golden Rules You Should Live By When Combining Fonts: Tips From a Designer," by Jamie Kliever. Read the entire article: https://designschool.canva.com/blog/combining-fonts-10-must-know-tips-from-a-designer/

Step 3: Upload logos and images

Finally, to complete your Brand Kit, you'll upload your brand's photos, logos, and graphics so they are easily accessible across all of your team's projects. You can always add to this library of images, and they'll be available to you your team when they are creating or remixing designs.

What do you need?

Graphics files to be used across your brand graphics (such as logos)

What do you need to do?

1 Open up the **Brand Kit tab** under the Your Brand tab in your Canva for Work account

2 Upload graphics files into **Logos** section in your Brand Kit

3 Done!

To upload a file, simply click on the + under the Logos section and you'll be prompted to choose a file from your local hard drive.

A preview of the file will appear there when uploading is complete. To use these brand graphics when you're working on a project, click on the arrow icon in the left navigation tabs to access the Logos folder. From here you can click on or drag and drop any image to place it into your design. Whenever the Logo folder is updated in your Brand Kit, the updates will be reflected here for every team member.

Canva provides a treasure trove of image tools that can help you be more productive and create beautiful brand-consistent designs. Here are the top 4 image tools that will keep your team out of Photoshop and cranking out beautiful designs, fast:

Crop and resize photos

You can do this right inside of Canva -- just double click on an image and use the handles to resize; drag the image around to crop. Click on the checkmark to accept your edits or the X to cancel.

Apply filters, save a custom filter for reuse

Applying a consistent filter to images can help you create a visually consistent brand on social media. Canva makes this easy by allowing you either use a preset filter or to save your own custom preset as a Filter Code. To

grab the code, select a photo, click on Filter, and select Advanced Options. There you can tweak your filter using the sliders until it's just right -- then copy the Filter Code to use later. Share this Filter Code with your team, and they can apply it to all of your social media photos for a distinctive and recognizable feeling to your brand.

Choose from thousands of free images, icons, and layouts

You don't have to design all of your brand's graphics from scratch. Easily access a huge and growing library of free images and graphics right in Canva that you can use in your brand's designs. (Remember that if you use an element from Canva's library that requires payment, you will need to pay $1 every time that image is used in a design.)

Get your images organized

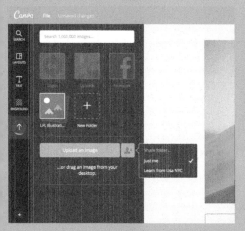

Centralize your graphics and photos into folders, then share the folders with your team to easily grant them access.

Did you know this SVG secret?

If you upload SVG graphics, you can change their colors right in Canva -- no need to open up the source file in a graphics program!

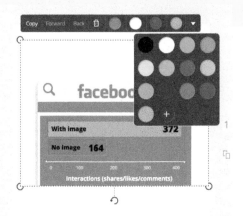

What types of files can I upload?

To upload to Canva, files must be JPEG, PNG or SVG format. Use PNG for graphics with transparent backgrounds. The file needs to be under 25MB using the RGB colorspace. At this time, CMYK colorspace is not supported.

With all of your graphic elements in place for your brand, it's time to really have some fun (and get productive) -- by creating brand templates for your team!

Chapter 4
Creating your Brand's Templates

You're about to supercharge your team's productivity

When it comes to efficiency and preserving the purity of your brand, templates are the real power of Canva for Work. If your Canva for Work Brand Kit is the skeleton, the "bones" of your brand -- your Templates are the muscle! By using these remixable layouts, you'll be able to create consistent branded designs faster than ever before.

Templates matter because – deadlines

You can give your team the fonts, colors, and graphics they need -- but it's the arrangement and layout of those elements that's often the most time-consuming. And time for trial and error is not something most businesses have in abundance.

All too often we find ourselves relying on one person or a small, often overworked department of graphic designers to make beautiful branded designs when we need them. And we usually need them NOW!

So, the people in the trenches (who are very often non-designers) cobble together something "that will work." Or they'll have to wait until the designer can get to the project, often missing a critical window of opportunity.

What if designers and the people who need them were able to work together seamlessly to create consistent designs, quickly and easily? With templates in Canva for Work, you can. Designers can do what they do best - craft the look and feel of your brand's visual marketing. And the rest of your team can do what they do best - create awesome content for those designs.

Fewer decisions, faster work

The way things used to be...

Early in my career I worked as an in-house designer at a print shop. We designed and printed a lot of newsletters for our clients. I loved those projects because I could knock them out quickly. For each one, we had a manila folder. Taped to the folder were the chips for each color used, and inside you'd find the last issue of the newsletter along with the content for that month's issue (usually text on a floppy disk back in those days). I'd open up the template for the newsletter, drop everything in, and send it to the back for printing. Having a template made production quick and easy!

This is why this next step is so important to getting your team ready to create beautiful visuals with Canva for Work. You've given them the colors, fonts, and art, but you need to show them what to do with them and how to put it all together. Provide them with well-designed drag-and-drop templates they can customize and your brand visual workflow will be bulletproof!

Do the work now, save time later

In Canva for Work, you can create a template for virtually any type of print or web project. From brochures to infographics, invitations to presentations — your team has all their content needs covered. They can use the templates as-is, with simple copy edits, or use it as a starting point and change text, images, photo filters, and add pages, for example. By doing the design work up front and creating all of the templates you'll want to use, you'll be able to keep all of your designs consistent and on-brand.

You can create templates either from a new design or from an existing project in Your Designs. Let's begin with the first method, creating a template from scratch, followed by making an existing design into a template. Then I'll show you the magic of the Magic Resize feature for automatically creating several formats at once (spoiler: you're going to love it!)

How to create a template from a new design

What do you need?

Start by creating a list of marketing materials your team needs most often (e.g. Instagram posts, Presentations, email headers,

Pinterest graphics, etc.). You'll also need your business's brand style guide so you can create template designs for each that are consistent with your brand. Now pick one to get started. In this exercise, we'll create an Instagram Post.

NOTE *Templates can be created by team members with Administrator or Template Designer designations. If your account level is Member, you'll be able to create designs using templates, but not create templates. To find out more about account types and what each can and cannot do, jump ahead to the next chapter!*

What do you need to do?

1. Open up the Templates tab under the Your Brand tab in your Canva for Work account

2. Click on the **Add a New Template** button

3. Choose a format for your new template

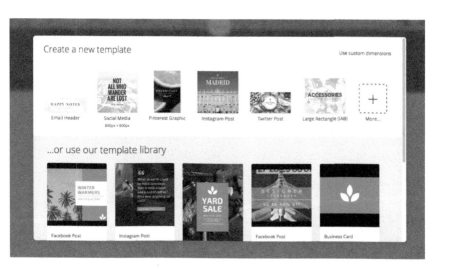

④ From here, you can start adding elements to the canvas, or choose an existing project from Your Designs to bring in some commonly-used elements to get you started. I have several formats that use my email header here, so I'll select one to bring it into my design.

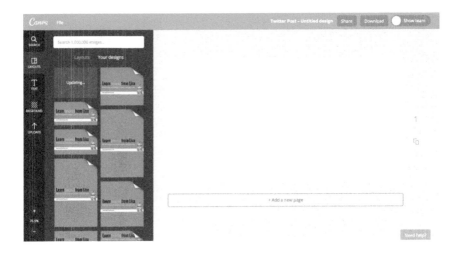

⑤ I'll add some elements here – a quote, my avatar illustration, and a URL. Once your design is complete, give it a name by clicking on the name at the top of the screen

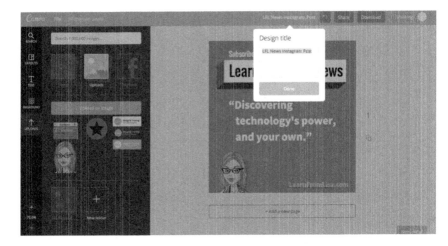

6 Click Show Team and check the box to **Publish as a Template**

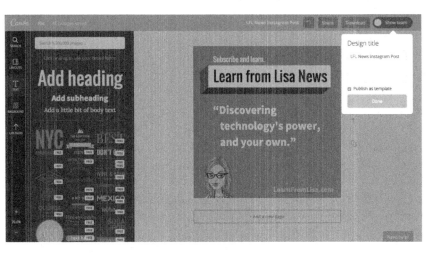

7 Done! The template will now appear under your brand's templates and will be available to your whole team to use and remix.

Productivity Tip:

To find out the format and dimensions of a design you're working on, click on the File menu in the upper left hand corner of the screen.

How to make a template from an existing design

You're going to love how easy this is! If you have a design that you use often, it's very simple to make it into a template in Canva for Work, making it available to all of your team members to reuse and remix. Here's how.

What do you need?

Select a design from Your Designs. I'll choose the Social media quote.

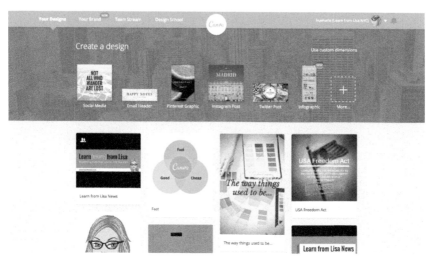

What do you need to do?

1. The design will open in a new window in the Canva editor.

2. Just click on Show Team in the upper right corner of the screen and check the box to **Publish as a Template**.

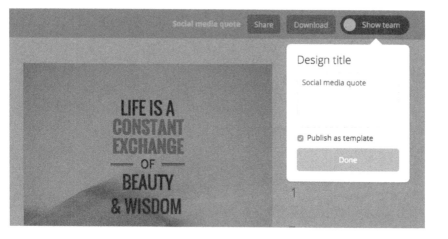

3 Done! You've just shared the design as a template, and anyone on your team can reuse it and remix it to create their own consistent, beautifully branded designs.

Tips for great templates

⭐ Consistent image filter codes, type spacing, transparency, logo placement.

⭐ Look at past posts and projects to be sure you take into account the typical length of copy your team will need to put into the template.

⭐ Consider creating and following a style guide for your brand's visual marketing materials. You should always use the same fonts, sizes, colors, and image types. Canva Design School has a primer on creating one for your blog here. (http://lisa.fyi/blogstyleguide)

For more tips on creating a consistent look and feel throughout all of your templates, see The Art of a Consistent Brand Image on the Canva Design School (http://lisa.fyi/brandimage)

How to create multiple template formats using the magic of Magic Resize

If you have a design that you want to repeat across multiple formats, creating a whole set of consistently branded templates, you're going to love the Magic Resize feature in Canva for Work.

Here's how you use the Magic Button to make multiple sizes of your design with one click.

What do you need?

A design that you want to replicate in multiple formats.

What do you need to do?

1. After opening your design in Canva for Work, click the **File** button on top of the page and choose **Magic Resize.**

2. Choose the sizes that you like and hit the **Abracadabra - Resize!** button.

3. The new formats will open up in different tabs with different sizes.

4. Make adjustments to your design as necessary to ensure that the placement of text and images is optimized for the new format.

5. Rename each format so you can easily identify them. As of this writing, the default is the name of the source design (which can get really confusing!)

While you may find that the new formats will still need some design tweaking here and there, you'll find that this button can truly work magic to save you time in creating consistent designs.

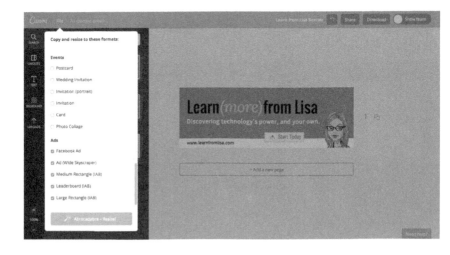

The Magic Resize feature is especially helpful in creating banners in various sizes. With a few adjustments here and there, you'll have a consistent banner campaign in no time!

How can I tell if an image is free or paid?

Paid images are clearly labelled in the Canva library. To see if an image is free or costs US $1, roll your mouse over it in the Editor. You can use it for both personal or commercial use. With this One Time Use License you are paying to use the image in the one design. The license is much cheaper than traditional stock photography, however you'll need to make any changes to your design within 24 hours to avoid paying for the license again.

Remember, if you use a paid image in a template, you will be charged each time that image is used in a design.

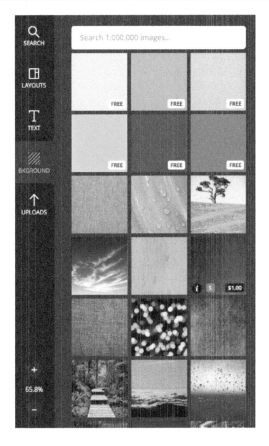

Need to give presentations? Create a template for that!

To build beautiful presentations, you can create a branded template for your team in Canva for Work so they can simply swap in their content and start presenting!

1 Select the size of the slides. Canva offers 2 different sizes for you to choose from: Standard (4:3 aspect ratio) or Widescreen (16:9 aspect ratio).

2 Choose the layout types you'd like your team to use. Consider the amount of text and images you'll want on the screen while presenting at any given time. You'll want to make several types of slides given that different presentations may require more visuals than another whereas a different presentation may need bulleted lists or full-blown paragraphs. Create a variety so that your team can easily pick and choose the layout they need.

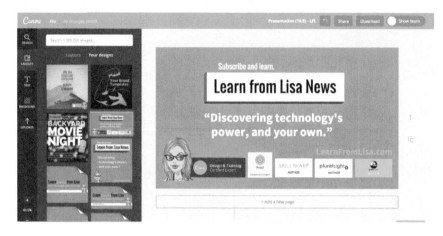

I chose to use one of my existing designs as a starting point, then arranged the elements to look more like a presentation.

3. Select the background you want for your slides. Make sure you consider your brand colors and overall style so that you choose a background aligned with your brand. Or if you don't want a background at all but would prefer on-brand images, look through Canva's awesome image gallery with free and premium options. Be sure to choose images that are on-brand and convey what you're trying to communicate for that particular slide.

Sample presentation slide template

BONUS! *I've created this reusable, remixable template for you to have your Brand Kit colors and fonts available at a glance. To use it for free in Canva for Work, log into your account and go to:*

http://www.lisa.fyi/brand-kit-template

This will open a copy of the sample template shown here. You can then customize the content with your colors and fonts. Print out and share with your team!

COMPANY

Learn From Lisa

LOGO

Headings - Oswald

Subheadings - Source Sans Pro

Body Text - Lora

#F16300
PRIMARY

#F9AB00
PRIMARY

#A0BF35
SECONDARY

#94C4CE
SECONDARY

#00727C
SECONDARY

Made by LearnFromLisa.com

MADE IN *Canva* for Work

CHAPTER 5

Exporting, Sharing, and Collaborating with Your Team

In Canva, you can share your designs with your clients for approval, with your colleagues for accolades, and with your friends for fun. You can even share an editable link so that others can work with you on a design. But when you have a brand image to protect and many hands in the pot (some designers, some not) you may find you need more control over the collaborative process. This is where Canva for Work shines.

In this chapter I'll introduce you to the advanced collaboration features in Canva for Work, and walk you through team account management, how to share designs and work on them together, and finally how to export files. I'll go on to explain the various formats and the important difference between web and print graphics.

Supercharged team collaboration features in Canva for Work

In Canva for Work, you can go beyond simply sharing editable designs. It's built to really streamline the way you work together, allowing you to:

 Create brand templates

⭐ Share photo folders with your team

⭐ Share designs in your private Team Stream

⭐ Control team members' account levels and access

One of the best new features is the ability to create your own team, adding people with different levels of access -- administrators, template designers, and members. This is great if you're working with a designer; s/he can create templates and save them right in your brand kit for your whole team to use.

Canva for Work User roles

Administrators
Can manage your team members, create design templates for your brand, and edit your brand kit.

 Template designers
Can create design templates for your brand and edit your brand kit. Invite your designers and we'll send them special tips to get started.

 Members
Can create and share designs. Perfect for anyone who needs to make branded designs — especially your colleagues in marketing, social media & sales.

Another killer feature for teams is the Team Stream. In the standard free Canva tool, you can use the Stream to share your designs with the world, allowing any Canva user to like or comment on your designs. With Canva for Work, the Stream is restricted to your own Team Members so you can see what your team is creating and like or comment on their designs. Of course, you can always publicly share your Canva for Work designs once they're ready for the world.

Maintaining the purity of your brand is much easier in Canva for Work. By sharing photos, logos, brand templates, and other custom assets, you can be sure that everyone has the visual elements they need – ready to drag and drop.

Managing Your Team

Anyone on your team can invite other people to become a team member. Administrators can set individual roles, forming an organized flow that will keep everyone working together efficiently and effectively.

Within a team, administrators can assign the role of Template Designer, giving that person the ability to create visual content templates for use by the team, and set up the Brand Kit. Members can help contribute to projects, adding design elements and making edits.

You can add anyone with a Canva account to your team. If you choose a monthly billing plan, the rate is US $12.95 a month for each person. If you choose an annual plan, the price per person is US $9.95 a month (which is a more than 20% discount).

	Administrator	Template Designer	Team Member
Create designs and share them to the Team Stream	X	X	X
Use the team Brand Kit to create consistent designs	X	X	X
Use team Templates to rapidly create custom designs	X	X	X
Upload and share photo folders	X	X	X
Transform designs between different design types with Magic Resize	X	X	X
Invite new team members	X	X	X
Edit Brand Kit colors and fonts	X	X	
Create, edit, and delete team layouts	X	X	
Add and remove team members and assign roles	X		
Control billing and subscription info	X		

HOW TO ADD TEAM MEMBERS

While any member can invite new team members, Administrators have the power to add and remove them, and set their roles on the team. If anyone but an Administrator invites someone, they can only set their permissions to their level or lower. For example: an Admin can invite another Admin, a Template Designer can invite other Template Designers or Members, and Members can only invite other Members.

To access the list of team members, invite members, and set roles, go to **Your Brand** tab, then click on the **Team Members** tab.

HOW TO REMOVE TEAM MEMBERS

Click on the **role menu** next to the name of the member you want to remove and click the option marked **Remove from team**.

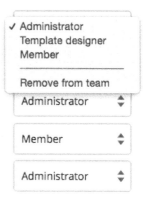

WHAT HAPPENS TO A DESIGNER WHEN THEY'RE REMOVED FROM A TEAM?

First, they'll no longer be able to switch to the team account to access brand content or templates. Secondly, the designer will lose access to the designs they created as part of the team. **However**, other members of the team will continue to have access to any template designs the removed designer previously created. If you'd like to add the person to your team once again, they'll regain access to the designs they created as part of your team.

Sharing and Collaboration

Canva for Work allows you to share designs and assets with your team, and then share your finished designs with the world. Let's look at the ways you can share.

SHARING ASSETS WITH YOUR TEAM

With Canva for Work, you can create folders and organize your uploaded photos to make them accessible to your entire team. Here's how.

1. Go to **Your Designs** and start a new design.

2. Go to the **Uploads** tab and click the **New Folder** button to create a new folder.

③ Click on the folder title to edit.

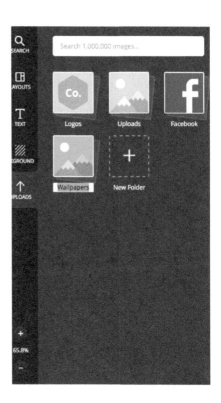

④ Click the **Upload an image** button to upload new images into the folder. You can also drag images from your desktop onto the folder to upload them. You can shift-select images to upload multiple files at once.

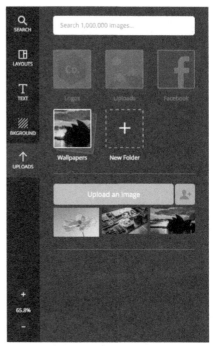

5 To share the folder with
your whole team, click the
share button next to the
Upload an image button.

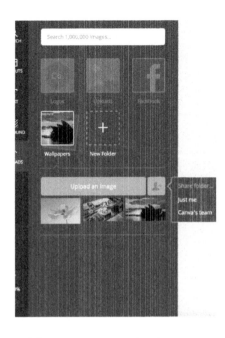

Now everyone on your team will have access to the images
to use in their designs!

To see what other people on your team are designing, you
can check out your **Team Stream**. This stream works just like
the Canva community design stream for personal accounts,
where you can view, like, and comment on other designs,
except your Team Stream will only feature designs made and
shared by those on your Canva for Work team. Here's how to
view your team design stream:

1 First, make sure that you're logged into your team account.
To switch to your team account, click the **account button**

58

located in the upper right-hand corner of the **Your Designs** screen, then choose your team account.

Next, click the **stream** button at the top of your screen to view your Team Stream. Just like in the Canva community design stream you'll be able to like and comment on designs in the stream, which only the other members of your team will be able to view.

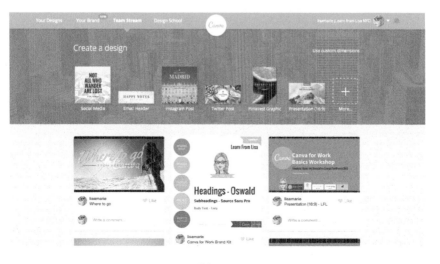

SHARING DESIGNS WITH YOUR TEAM

You can add your own designs to the Team Stream by clicking on the privacy button on the top right-hand corner of the design screen. While you're logged into your team account, it will read **Show team.**

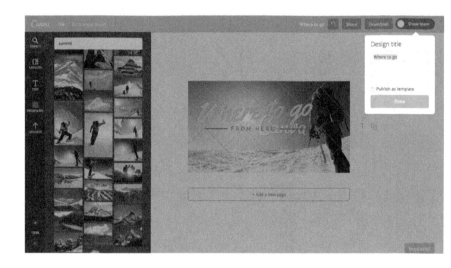

When toggled on and shared in your Team Stream, it will read **Showing.**

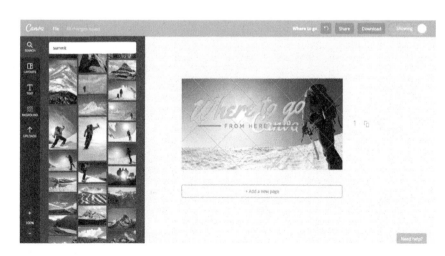

Sharing designs on social media

If you'd like to share beyond your team and show the design to the world, click on the Share button on the top right-hand corner of the design screen.

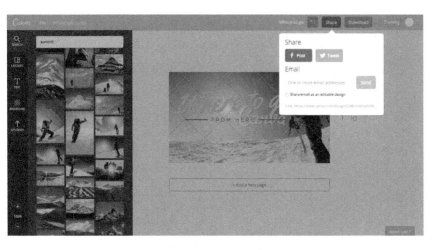

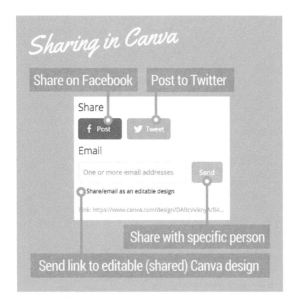

From here, you have several ways to let others view and comment on your design:

- Share on Facebook

- Post to Twitter

- Share with a specific person via email

- Optionally send link to the editable Canva design via email. The recipient will need a Canva account to make edits, and you'll see their edits next time you open the design in Canva.

As you can see, social sharing is built in to Canva, making it easy to collaborate and get your brand graphics seen by the world.

Exporting Files

After you've created your visual content, be it a poster, infographic, presentation, etc. you can download the finished design to your hard drive in various formats. Your design will no longer be floating "in the cloud" but will actually be a file that you can share with others, send to your printer, or even share online via services like Slideshare or Instagram. But to ensure your designs look their best, you need to make sure you choose the right type of file to download.

*If your design uses any **premium elements**, you'll be asked to pay for them when you download your file. If you have any pre-purchased credits remaining, click the **pay & download button** to spend them. Otherwise, enter your credit card information to pay for the elements in your design and click the **make payment button**. Did you catch a mistake or need to make any changes? You can continue to edit and download your design without paying again for premium elements for 24 hours after your initial download.*

For Print

If you're printing your design from a home printer or sending it to a print professional, you should download a PDF file with high-quality images. Canva exports PDF for print at a maximum resolution of 300 DPI.

Your design's resolution refers to how many pixels are displayed on screen or how much ink is used in a print. If you need to create a design with a certain DPI, this refers to resolution as well (DPI stands for "dots per inch").

Downloading your design as a PDF is quick and easy. When your design is ready, click the **download button**, and then choose the button marked **PDF: For Print**. Your file will automatically begin downloading. Depending on your browser's preferences, you'll either be prompted to select a download location, or the file will automatically be saved to your downloads folder. Then you'll be ready to go to press!

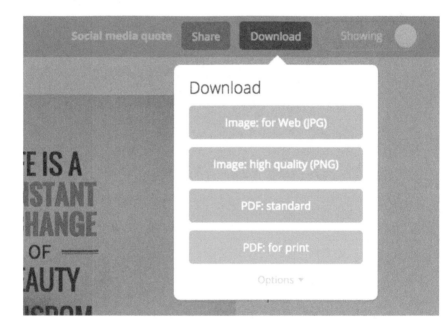

If your design has a background that goes to the edges (full bleed) and you're going to have it printed, you'll want to include crop marks in the PDF. Crop marks indicate where your design should be trimmed so that your prints have crisp, clean color or image that goes all the way to the edge of the paper.

To create a PDF with crop marks and extra bleed over the edges, click the **Download** button and then the options arrow to display more options. Next, check the box to **Publish with crop marks & bleed**, and then download your PDF. The file you download will now have little black lines showing you (or your print professional) where to trim.

Image showing crop marks and bleed for printing to the edges of the paper.

Export for web

To export your design for use on the web, you can choose PNG or JPG format.

Both JPG and PNG files are great for publishing designs on the web. They download at 96 dpi, which will look sharp and crisp on most computer displays. They are also relatively small in size, so they're perfect for emailing and posting online.

Here are some good rules of thumb when choosing between PNG and JPG formats:

- ✪ JPG files are better if there are photos or gradients in your design

- ✪ PNG files are better for flat colors, illustrations and crisp typography. You also have the option to save PNG files with a transparent background.

When you're ready to download a web-ready version of your design, follow the instructions I've provided for downloading a PDF and choose JPG or PNG as the format. The file will download to your hard drive and you can use it however you like!

How to export a transparent image

With Canva for Work, you can create designs with transparent backgrounds. This has been a much-requested feature, and is

If you plan to upload your design to Instagram, be sure to export as a JPG file. If you post a PNG, Instagram will automatically convert it to JPG for posting, often resulting in excessive compression which makes the image look blurry.

especially helpful for logos and illustrations where you may want to layer the design on top of other elements, photos, or colored backgrounds. Here's how it's done:

1 Create a design using any format. IMPORTANT: Don't add a background to the design.

2 After creating your design, click the **Download** button.

3 Click **Options** at the bottom of the **Download** menu. Check the box to **Make the Background Transparent** and then export the design as a PNG.

4 Now you will have a transparent PNG file that you can use with any color background!

Share and share alike

As you can see, Canva makes it easy to collaborate with your team, and share your designs online and off. It also takes the guesswork out of formats and resolution, letting you concentrate on creating beautiful content.

Chapter 6
Where to Go From Here

At this point, you should be well on your way to setting up a workflow in Canva for Work that supports your team and your brand. As you discover more about Canva for Work (and hopefully even have some fun creating designs!) you'll find you'll want to further expand your skills and stay up to date with the latest features and news.

To help guide you, I've put together this shortlist of valuable resources for best practices, helpful tips, and inspiration.

Canva Design School –
https://designschool.canva.com/

Canva YouTube Channel –
https://www.youtube.com/user/canvadesign

Free Intro to Canva Course on Skillshare –
http://www.lisa.fyi/learn-canva-ss

Canva on Twitter –
https://twitter.com/canva

Canva on Facebook –
http://facebook.com/canva

Canva on Instagram –
https://instagram.com/canva/

Canva on Pinterest –
https://www.pinterest.com/canva/

@Lisamarienyc on twitter –
http://twitter.com/lisamarienyc

And for the most up-to-date resources and book content updates go to **http://learnfromlisa.com/ready-set-brand/** where I'll post all the latest links and announcements. Be sure to join my mailing list and community there. I'd love to hear your feedback and experiences with Canva.

Thanks for joining me for this whirlwind tour of Canva for Work. I hope you're feeling empowered to create, and that this book becomes your trusted reference.

Happy designing!

Acknowledgements

I vowed back in 2007 after writing my first book, **Flash Video for Professionals,** that I'd never. write. another. book. EVER. Yet here we are.

It's all Canva's fault, really. When I realized how many people could be empowered by it, that it could remove barriers to communication for so many people —well, I just couldn't help myself. It needed to be written. And I certainly didn't do it alone!

First I want to thank my right-hand woman, Martina Kunar, for her diligent research, copywriting, editing, and for holding down the fort with our consulting clients during our whirlwind production schedule. Thanks also to Michelle Racca for her production support. And huge gratitude to the talented Amber Medel for design and layout of the book. We couldn't have pulled it all together without her positive attitude, always on-point design and superhuman turnaround time!

This book certainly would not be in your hand (or on your screen) without the support and resources generously provided by the Canva team—Anna Guerrero, Andre Pinantoan, Zach Kitschke, and graciously headed up by Hannah Field, with invaluable support from founder Melanie Perkins. Hannah and Anna, this book would not have been possible without your frank feed-back that always pushed me to make the book better and more useful. Thank you!

A big thank you to Canva's Chief Evangelist and social media powerhouse Guy Kawasaki for his support in spreading the word about this book—and for encouraging me to create it. With his ebook APE: Author, Publisher, Entrepreneur–How to Publish an Ebook, he provided a guiding force as I put this together (and BTW, I wrote this book because of Good Reason #1!) I've also been deeply inspired by his book Enchantment to do more to create better experiences for people (and to keep smiling).

And finally, I'm eternally grateful to, and for, my ever-patient husband Tom. Along with our daughter, they've been amazing through nights and weekends of "mommy's working". . . Now, let's go to Disney World?!

Lisa Larson-Kelley

About the Author

Lisa Larson-Kelley is a passionate trainer and sought-after speaker at technology conferences worldwide, with courses published with lynda.com, Skillshare, and Pluralsight. Her consultancy, Kelley Green Consulting, provides marketing support to clients including Google, Adobe, and Microsoft along with many smaller start-ups. Lisa's passion is empowering people to embrace technology and see its power—and their own. Sign up for her mailing list for updates at BeginnersBrain. com, and follow her on twitter @lisamarienyc.

Kelley Green Consulting gives individuals and companies the knowledge and tools to navigate change.

Get your team ready to hit the ground running with beautiful designs. Our mission is to help people make the most of technology—and as one of Canva's official experts, we can help you and your company make the most of Canva. Learn how to maximize your design and workflow—keeping your teams in sync and your design on brand. Offering training and design services to companies large and small. Contact team@kelleygreenconsulting.com to find out how we can help you and your team.

CPSIA information can be obtained
at www.ICGtesting.com
Printed in the USA
BVOW05s0226270317
479523BV00022B/372/P